God's Word is perfect and
makes simple people wise!
Psalm 19:7

ISBN: 979-8-9922853-4-5 - Paperback

ISBN: 979-8-9922853-5-2 - Hardcover

NBeirene Press

GOD'S WORD IS...

Written by Nancy Owusu Adu

GOD'S WORD IS A LAMP

A lamp that shines in darkness.
God's word guides my steps and
shows me the way. I can't get lost!

Your word is a lamp to my feet,
and a light for my path
Psalm 119:105 WEB

GOD'S WORD IS SWEETER THAN HONEY

Honey is sweet but God's Word is sweeter
and far better!
It makes my life sweet
and helps me grow!

Your words are sweet to me,
they are sweeter than honey.
Psalm 119:103

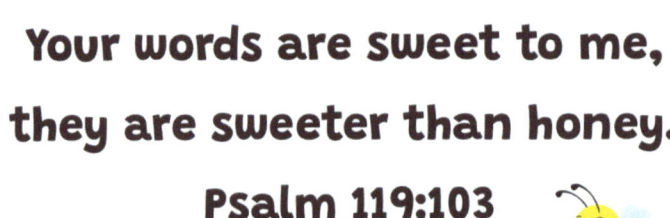

GOD'S WORD IS BETTER THAN GOLD

Gold is valuable.

God's word is more valuable and precious!

It gives me riches and wisdom.

God's word is far more precious than gold,

even the finest gold. Psalm 19:10

GOD'S WORD IS LIKE A HAMMER

A hammer is strong and powerful.

Like a hammer, God's word is strong and able to break through difficult problems in my life.

God's Word is like a hammer that breaks a rock in pieces. Jeremiah 23:29

GOD'S WORD IS
A MIRROR

A mirror shows me what I look like.
Like a mirror God's Word shows me what
I need to fix and helps me get better!

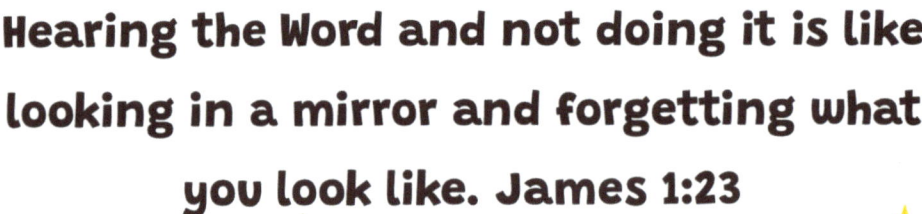

Hearing the Word and not doing it is like

looking in a mirror and forgetting what

you look like. James 1:23

GOD'S WORD IS A SEED

A seed grows to produce a great harvest. Like a seed, God's Word can grow and produce lots of fruits in my life!

And the seed that fell on good soil produced 100 times more crops. The seed is the Word of God. Luke 8:8 and 11

GOD'S WORD IS LIKE FIRE

Fire burns and destroys. Like fire, the word of God can burn away all the bad stuff in my life and make me better!

God's Word is like a great fire. Jeremiah 23:29

GOD'S WORD IS LIKE WATER

Water washes and cleanses.
Like water, God's Word washes away my
sin and makes me clean again!

He makes me clean by the washing of
water with the word. Ephesians 5:26

GOD'S WORD IS MEDICINE

Medicine heals.

God's word is medicine to my whole body.

It heals me from head to toe and

everywhere in between!

God's word is life and health to all your

body. Proverbs 4:22

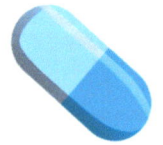

GOD'S WORD IS SHARPER THAN A SWORD

A sword is a weapon used in battle.

God's word is a weapon against the enemy.

It defeats the devil every time!

God's Word is sharper than a two-edged sword. Hebrews 4:12

GOD'S WORD IS ALIVE

It is living and continues to grow every day! It works in me and has power to change me from the inside out!

God's Word is alive and powerful.

Hebrews 4:12

GOD'S WORD IS LIFE

It brings life to any hopeless situation
and gives life to everyone who believes.
To find God's Word is to find life!

Finding God's word is like finding life and
receiving favor from God. Proverbs 8:35

www.ingramcontent.com/pod-product-compliance
Lightning Source LLC
Chambersburg PA
CBHW041609120626
46551CB00002B/375